Investing in the stock market for beginners and experts, earn money on the Internet from home:

2 5 tips for investing in stock markets

© Antonio Robinhood

© C. and C. Editions

Content

1 Buy as if you were never going to sell. But take advantage of volatility and growth to withdraw profits (sell)

2 Avoid trading and working with brokers who have been reported

3 Look for companies that pay dividends, are not expensive and have a future

4 Look for growth opportunities

5 Avoid trading financial derivatives

6 Invest by diversifying by sector

7 Also diversify within each sector

8 Invest periodically, without feelings

9 Balance your portfolio by scaling positions

10 Do not invest money that you will need

11 Don't get obsessed with the day to day of the stock market

12 Avoid commissions

13 You have to be prepared to see your portfolio drop 50% and not panic

14 Ignore most news and recommendations

15 be patient

16 Learn from experience

17 Do not close positions with losses

18 Have your own philosophy as an investor, which is solid, although it can be flexible

19 Choose asymmetric risk situations

20 Don't try to understand the market or expect it to be rational

21 Choose companies that lead their sectors or that have competitive advantages

22 Enjoy the process

23 Follow your instincts

24 Don't forget about taxes

25 Share what you learn

Other books that can help you find opportunities in the stock market in which to invest

1 Buy as if you were never going to sell. But take advantage of volatility and growth to withdraw profits (sell)

The classic buy and hold is a strategy that focuses on the long term, I do too, but I make sales and to enjoy the money and reinvest balancing my portfolio.

That is, buy as if you were never going to sell, but if prices rise above what you consider to be their value or, being less subjective, if you have already achieved a revaluation of at least 30%, consider starting to sell Actions. If they do not charge you a lot of commissions for trading, they may not be all at once, if it keeps going up, you keep selling, and if it goes down a lot, you buy more.

I like to get money from time to time, to see that I am not only aiming for future benefits. It sounds like I am speculating, but actually I don't, because I invest in assets that I trust for the long term.

I know the market is very volatile (some more than others) and I withdraw profits when it is high.

It all also depends on the type of shares you choose (you can read about it in *Investing in the stock market 2020 2021)*, if they are growth shares, the number of operations I do is even greater, I sell before that if they were dividends.

Growth stocks (those that do not distribute dividends) will only generate a real economic benefit if you sell them (or that they begin to distribute dividends at some point.

2 Avoid trading and work with brokers who have been reported

There are brokers that invest a lot in advertising, but then sell the orders of their users to link them with orders from other clients of theirs. How is this? Large purchases and sales generate volatility, if a mutual fund (for example) wants to sell many shares and want the price to be the maximum, it will need to find a broker that will get the opposite orders (to buy) for the highest possible quote.

Before making an account with a broker, Google their name next to the word scam and complaints. The same when you think about reading a book or buying a course on how to trade.

Some of *Youtubers* most famous even recognize, do not know if with pride but I think so, having spent years losing money until you find the "formula" to win.

The statistics speak for themselves, if you trade intraday (on the same day) with financial derivatives, you will most likely lose money. If you buy stocks and hold long enough, it is safer than Aum bodies your equity (and how to succeed or on the stock to Wall Street).

Forget short-term operations based on density, stick with strong hands and other stories to live effortlessly overnight. The bag returns money, but you must have a lot for it to give you enough back.

3 Look for companies that distribute dividends, are not expensive and have a future

Some of this type, which have been in my portfolio for a long time and I have taken advantage of the fact that they are trading at very low prices to increase positions are: AT&T, Telefónica, Gilead Science and Barrick Gold. They are four very important companies that distribute a juicy dividend and do not trade very high. They have a future because their markets, in which they have a privileged position, have a future.

Telecommunications (AT&T and Telefónica) have benefited enormously from the confinement, we have seen the need to use telephones, Internet, and online entertainment more than ever, and that is an economic benefit for these companies.

4 Look for growth opportunities

Here I mean the so-called *small caps: small-cap* companies. In other words, with great growth potential. They also carry high risk, but heck, you only live once.

I am not telling you to invest your entire portfolio, not even most of it, I allocate approximately 20% and, the truth is, I am having magnificent results, as with Aurora Cannabis.

5 Avoid or stop with financial derivatives

I already mentioned it, I told you to avoid unreliable trading and brokers. But I repeat, it is worth it.

Do not put your money into anything you don't understand, it's a basic rule made famous by W. Buffett.

Speculation is a lottery, you can use methods to control risk, but that is nothing more than limiting the amount you can lose daily so as not to ruin yourself the first day. The data is clear, many *traders* lose money.

6 Reverses diversifying sectorialmente

Think about your investment portfolio in sectors: tourism, telecommunications, mining, financial sector, real estate, catering, pharmaceutical or health sector, entertainment, services ...

The important thing is that, although a sector is doing badly, such as tourism, which with the pandemic has had to pay dividends and its price has dropped, nothing happens, because other sectors rise.

7 Also diversify within each sector

Invest distributing the capital to reduce risks, also within each sector there will be winners and losers.

For example, we all know that renewable energies are the future, that is why many of us have put money in shares of companies that have this business, and prices have risen, but what we do not know is finally which companies dominate the market and if any will go bankrupt. For this reason, I have sold my shares in companies like First Solar, SunPower and Maxeon Solar. I have already made good money from them and I don't want to lose it. Renova can continue to invest in energy b them (which is in line with my ethics and philosophy as an investor) without having to suffer the volatility of growth stocks-specul Ativas and getting dividends. I do it through Brookfield Asset Management, a Canadian multinational that, among other businesses, has assets in renewable energy. In this way my portfolio is diversified, and I am not afraid of the volatility of a still very speculative market, in which you can make money, a lot of money, but which can also make you lose it.

8 Invest periodically, without feelings

You may just want to move money that you have saved, but if you really want to be an investor, it is best to invest it all at once. Make investing a habit, like watering plants or feeding your pet.

You can allocate a fixed percentage of your income to the stock market, if you want security, focus on dividend stocks.

This will help you avoid volatility, although you can adapt your strategy to changes in the market. If some month the stock market is high and you do not find any opportunity, you can not invest or invest less capital, and when prices fall, take the opportunity to buy more.

The question is that you do it yes or yes. Only in that way will your portfolio grow, and you will not eat the profits, this is not incompatible with making withdrawals, just balance your accounts so that it makes sense.

9 Balance your portfolio by scaling positions

We have already mentioned it, but it deserves its own section.

A common practice in my trading is to sell some of the shares that have appreciated the most (usually I do not get rid of all of them at once) and, with that same money, buy more of those that have fallen in price since I bought.

If a company has appreciated above its target price (the price that you consider a target) you can sell a part of your position to withdraw profits. If it is a growth stock, do it without hesitation when there are movements of more than 50% revaluation, they are usually stocks with which there is much speculation so it is likely that it will fall quickly again (if it falls a lot, buy more) and maybe go up again later.

The escalations are also when the shares go down n, take the opportunity to buy more, that way, the average price of the shares will also be lower, and you can get away making money sooner.

10 Do not invest money that you will need

Invest because saving is losing money (inflation) and because the public pension system is not reliable; Invest for your financial freedom, not to pay the bills this month (you can do it, but you know, if you don't already know, that it is very risky. If you run out of money and have to go to credit, you will end up losing more money that if you had counted on the liquidity) .

The worst thing that can happen to you in the stock market is that you need the money, and your assets are below the price for which you bought them. You can only avoid this problem if it is money that you will not need, at least for a year. Better if it is never.

11 Don't get obsessed with the day to day of the stock market

Avoid wasting time constantly reviewing your stock price. It is good to check if there has been a large movement and an opportunity to sell: your shares have grown exaggerated due to some news, or purchase. a company has seen the price of its shares fall below its real value. No more.

12 Less commissions

Choose your broker very well. If your strategy is to only buy and hold, especially look at maintenance costs. If you like to speculate, buy, and sell growth stocks, check very well how much they charge for different brokers.

Never hire a pension plan or an actively managed investment fund. You will be paying so-called experts who have, in fact, historically performed very poorly. Better shape your own portfolio, nobody knows what the future will be, use logic and common sense, also train yourself by reading books like this one, but do not have in a box the financiers who work investing the money of others, on many occasions they do not the same with your own funds.

13 You have to be prepared to see your portfolio drop 50% and not panic

You need liquidity to take advantage of the drops and expand positions (buy more shares). Remember what W. Buffet says: "If you eat hamburgers every day, what do you prefer, does the price go up or down?" (Stocks are hamburgers if you are or aspire to be an investor).

If you have bought shares in a company and its price falls, you are happy, when it is around thirty percent, you take the opportunity to buy more. If it keeps going down, you keep buying, for example. with each drop of 10 or 20%.

14 Ignore most news and recommendations

I always remember the words of my teacher: Do not trust the advice to be rich of someone who is not rich.

If everyone is buying or doing something, this is not the time to buy or do it.

15 Be patient

The most days you will not have to do anything. The bag is wonderful because it makes your money work for you, do not ruin it working for your money.

Calm your investment, trust them, there will be days when lower prices, but this is a distance race, not a *sprint* .

16 Learn from experience

Both yours, and that of other investors you may know.

If you want to know my operations on the US and Spanish stock exchanges, I have published them so that everyone can learn from it, and I also enjoy learning what others have done. Although nothing is as effective as acting with your own money, you learn what to do because you do not want to lose a penny. And I can boast that I have never lost it, and if you follow the advice below, neither will you.

I have written some books that you can get for free with Kindle Unlimited or for a minimal investment buying them. I present them here:

A basic work is Learn to invest: What is investing and what are the types of assets .

If you are interested in starting new businesses, you cannot miss:

Business to make money from the coronavirus pandemic: The best proposals for financial success .

I have a trilogy about investing in the stock market, in Spanish and English, here are the links for the Spanish-speaking public:

Investing in the stock market 2020 2021: Strategy to make money with the coronavirus pandemic (Investments in the stock market with intelligence No. 1).

Investing in the Spanish stock market 2020 2021: Operation to make money with the coronavirus pandemic (Investments in the stock market with intelligence No. 2).

Invest in the Wall Street stock market (United States) (Updated was Biden and vaccine) 2020 2021: Operation to make money with the coronavirus pandemic ... in the stock market with intelligence No. 3).

17 Do not close positions with losses

Or what is the same: do not sell cheaper than what you bought. It is true that this advice could have exceptions, but they would mean that you have made a lot of mistakes when buying. It has never happened to me.

18 Have your own philosophy as Investor(a), it is solid, although it can be flexible

The important thing is that it allows you to remain calm in any context. What are you investing for? When you do, never think about the present, always do it in the future, how do you see it? Visualize the world in five years, a decade, a half century, which companies are the most important and why? Invest accordingly.

1 9 Choose asymmetric risk situations

That is, where what you can win is much more than what you can lose. Investing in the stock market is very attractive because, for example, you have shares that are worth one euro each, you can buy one hundred and in the worst case you will lose one hundred euros, in the best case, for example, that the price of each share rises to five euros, you will be earning five hundred. Five times more than the most you could have lost. The question is to have some indicator that it is possible to reach that price, such as that it has already arrived or that the prospects are very good.

20 Don't try to understand the market or expect it to be rational

Life is not to understand, it is to live. And the stock market is not for you to understand, it is for you to earn money with it (and companies get financing).

If you know that this company is worth it, do not worry because it is not yet reflected in its listing price, days, months, or years may pass, but most likely any day it will skyrocket.

21 Choose companies that lead their sectors or that have competitive advantages

Manger the trend, rather than the moment. Are you growing their regular benefits? Good sign to buy. Are they innovating? Another good news.

22 Enjoy the process

Unless your goal is exclusively retirement with dividends, withdraw benefits from time to time and have fun with the money.

23 Follow your instincts

It may seem wrong, but the truth is that instinct can tell us the result of a very complex cognitive processing, which we may not be aware of or able to rationalize, but which exists.

24 Don't forget about taxes

In making your calculations, do not forget the part that is going to take taxes to both dividends and sales of shares. Take it into account to know what net returns you are getting.

25 Share what you learn

Making money with the stock market is not difficult, you just must follow a strategy. I believe that anyone who has read this book will know how to get more out of their money than any investment fund, bonds, deposit or fixed place or other robbery-offer from your bank.

If this book has served you well, leave me a review on Amazon and share it so that we are more in the stock market, prices go up and we all get richer.

Disclaimer

Although the author has a college degree in Finance, this book does not amount to personalized financial advice. The work is limited to showing particular considerations linked to a specific experience. Just because something has happened does not mean it will happen again. In no case are we guaranteeing results.

The author and collaborators are not responsible for the consequences of implementing projects or actions motivated by this reading.

Links to Amazon are offered in the book, the author is affiliated with the company and could earn a small commission for what you buy after clicking. It is the same portal as if you enter from any other link .

Other books that can help you find opportunities in the stock market in which to invest

https://www.amazon.com/Amazon-defense-Response-manifesto-against-ebook/dp/B08TV9YVQ6/ref=sr_1_14?dchild=1&qid=1615462771&refinements=p_27%3AAntonio+Robinhood&s=digital-text&sr=1-14&text=Antonio+Robinhood

https://www.amazon.com/Investing-market-beginners-experts-Internet-ebook/dp/B08TVKHZHX/ref=sr_1_11?dchild=1&qid=1615462771&refinements=p_27%3AAntonio+Robinhood&s=digital-text&sr=1-11&text=Antonio+Robinhood

INVEST IN THE STOCK MARKET 2020-2021

STRATEGY FOR MAKING MONEY FROM THE CORONAVIRUS PANDEMIC

ANTONIO ROBINHOOD

C. y C.
crearycorregir.com
EDICIONES

https://www.amazon.com/Invest-stock-market-2020-Coronavirus-ebook/dp/B08P21ZG14/ref=sr_1_16?dchild=1&qid=1615462771&refinements=p_27%3AAntonio+Robinhood&s=digital-text&sr=1-16&text=Antonio+Robinhood

https://www.amazon.com/Investing-Spanish-stock-market-2020-ebook/dp/B08P53Z7RN/ref=sr_1_12?dchild=1&qid=1615462771&refinements=p_27%3AAntonio+Robinhood&s=digital-text&sr=1-12&text=Antonio+Robinhood

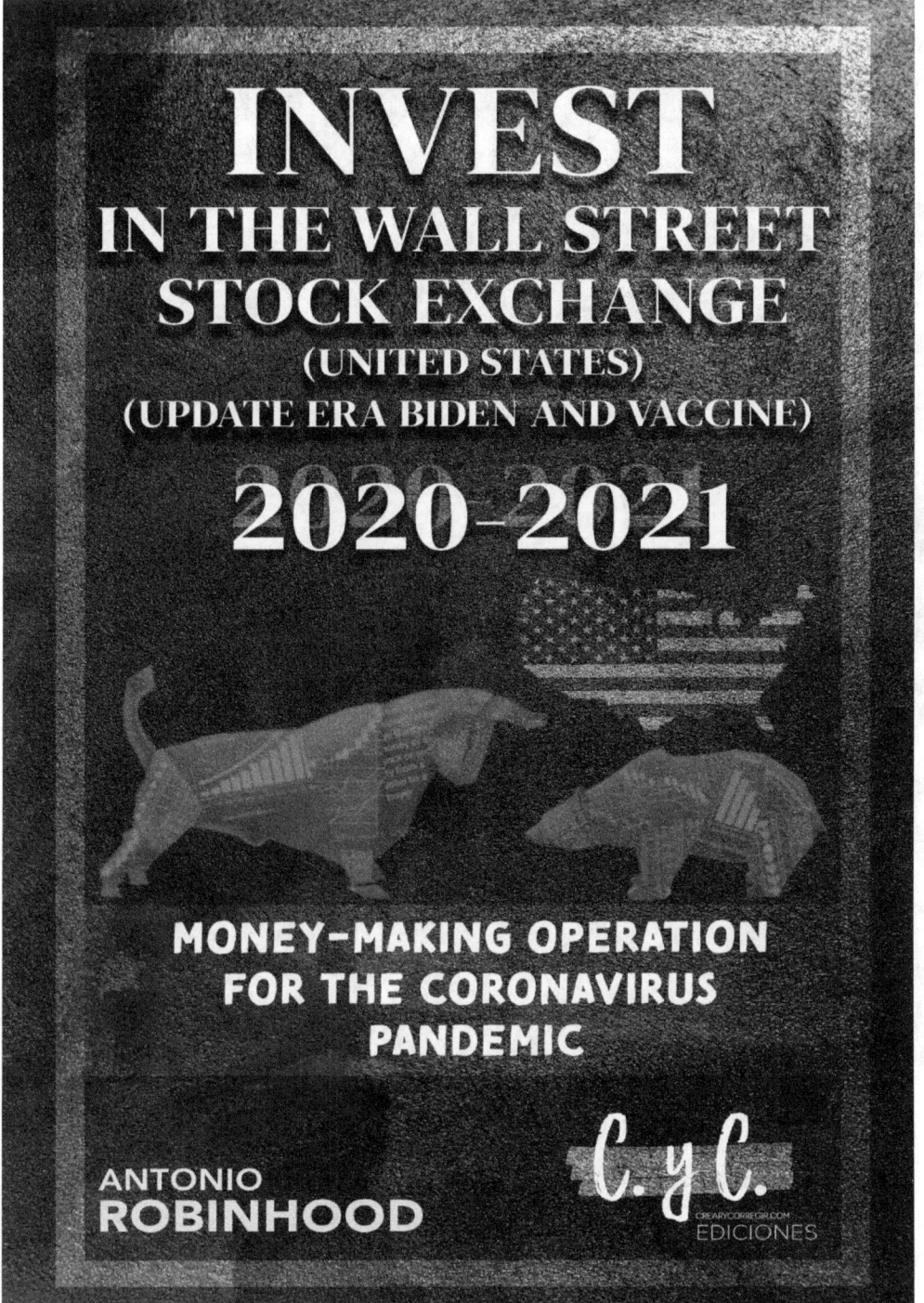

https://www.amazon.com/Invest-Street-Exchange-Updated-Vaccine-ebook/dp/B08P22BWM8/ref=sr_1_13?dchild=1&qid=1615462771&refinements=p_27%3AAntonio+Robinhood&s=digital-text&sr=1-13&text=Antonio+Robinhood

https://www.amazon.com/gp/product/B08Y94LS8C?pf_rd_r=0WGAYAHW5EKAXK CS3T8X&pf_rd_p=5ae2c7f8-e0c6-4f35-9071-dc3240e894a8&pd_rd_r=aae095aa-8d9a-4bbb-a949-3c7554516494&pd_rd_w=LjRlY&pd_rd_wg=ooIky&ref_=pd_gw_unk

INVESTING in DIVIDENDS

A guide to investing in the stock market and achieving financial freedom

ANTONIO ROBINHOOD

https://www.amazon.com/Investing-dividends-investing-achieving-financial-ebook/dp/B08Y837DL6/ref=sr_1_3?dchild=1&qid=1615462771&refinements=p_27%3AAntonio+Robinhood&s=digital-text&sr=1-3&text=Antonio+Robinhood

Translation from Spanish to English: Liliana Bogarín Cáceres.